Colorado

BY MARI KESSELRING

The Child's World®

Published by The Child's World®
1980 Lookout Drive • Mankato, MN 56003-1705
800-599-READ • www.childsworld.com

ACKNOWLEDGMENTS
The Child's World®: Mary Berendes, Publishing Director
The Design Lab: Design and production
Red Line Editorial: Editorial direction

PHOTO CREDITS: Jon Mullen/iStockphoto, cover, 1, 3; Matt Kania/Map Hero, Inc., 4, 5; Nick Lamb/Shutterstock, 7; Shutterstock, 9; Cindy Creighton/iStockphoto, 10; Don Fink/Shutterstock, 11; Ben Klaus/iStockphoto, 13; Photolibrary, 15; Doug Berry/iStockphoto, 17; Giuseppe Aresu/AP Images, 19; Nara Won/iStockphoto, 21; One Mile Up, 22; Quarter-dollar coin image from the United States Mint, 22

LIBRARY OF CONGRESS CATALOGING-IN-PUBLICATION DATA
Kesselring, Mari.
  Colorado / by Mari Kesselring.
    p. cm.
  Includes bibliographical references and index.
  ISBN 978-1-60253-450-6 (library bound : alk. paper)
  1. Colorado—Juvenile literature. I. Title.

F776.3.K47 2010
978.8—dc22

                    2010016167

Printed in the United States of America in Mankato, Minnesota.
July 2010
F11538

On the cover: The Rocky Mountains stretch more than 3,000 miles (4,828 km) across North America.

CONTENTS

Geography

Let's explore Colorado! Colorado is in the western United States.

WYOMING

NEBRASKA

UTAH

• Dinosaur

Steamboat
Springs •

• Greeley

Boulder •

Colorado River

Denver ★

COLORADO

Aspen •

Burlington

• Colorado Springs

Olathe •

Rocky Mountains

KANSAS

Pueblo •

La Junta •

Cortez • Mesa Verde
National Park

San Luis •

Trinidad •

NORTH
WEST   EAST
SOUTH

Antonito •

NEW MEXICO

OKLAHOMA

Cities

Denver is the capital of Colorado. It is the largest city in the state. Denver is high in the mountains. Aspen, Boulder, and Colorado Springs are other large cities in the state.

A nickname for Denver is "the Mile High City."

Denver is close to the Rocky Mountains. ▶

Land

Colorado is known for its high mountains. Part of the Rocky Mountains are in western Colorado. The state has **plateaus**. These are high, flat lands. Colorado also has rolling hills and **plains**. Many rivers run through the state.

Colorado means "colored" in Spanish. The Colorado River flows through reddish colored rocks.

The Rocky Mountains tower over a Colorado valley and river. ▶

Plants and Animals

Animals such as bears, beavers, and rabbits live in Colorado. The Colorado state bird is the lark bunting. This bird only lives in Colorado from April to September. It flies south for the winter. The state flower is the white and lavender Rocky Mountain columbine. This flower is so rare, it is against the law to pick more than 25 of the flowers a day.

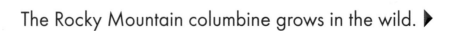

The Rocky Mountain columbine grows in the wild. ▶

The *Stegosaurus* is the Colorado state fossil. This dinosaur lived in the Colorado area 150 million years ago.

People and Work

About 5 million people live in Colorado. Most people live in cities. Many jobs are in **manufacturing**, mining, and **tourism**. Farming is also common in Colorado. Farmers grow corn, hay, and wheat.

A farmer hauls bales of hay in Boulder. ▶

History

Native Americans were the first people to live in Colorado. Later, people from Europe explored the area. The United States bought the land as part of the Louisiana Purchase in 1803. Colorado became the thirty-eighth state on August 1, 1876.

Some Native American tribes that have lived in Colorado are the Arapaho, the Cheyenne, and the Ute.

The Cheyenne, a Native American tribe, met with Colorado settlers in the 1800s. ▶

Ways of Life

Because of Colorado's many mountains, skiing and snowboarding are **popular** activities. Colorado has many ski **resorts** in the mountains.

Many people travel to Colorado to ski. ▶

Famous People

Condoleezza Rice attended school in Colorado. She was the secretary of state during the presidency of George W. Bush. Actor Tim Allen was born in Denver. Boxer Jack Dempsey was born in the state, too.

Condoleezza Rice attended the University of Denver. ▶

Famous Places

The cliff **dwellings** in Mesa Verde National Park are one interesting place to visit in Colorado. These are homes that people built in the rock a long time ago.

The Cliff Palace is one part of the cliff dwellings in Colorado. ▶

State Symbols

Seal

Two tools used for mining are in an X shape on Colorado's state seal. Go to childsworld.com/links for a link to Colorado's state Web site, where you can get a firsthand look at the state seal.

Flag

The *C* on Colorado's state flag stands for both Colorado and the state flower, the Rocky Mountain columbine.

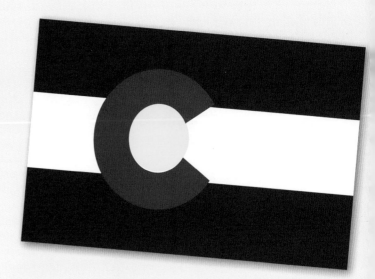

Quarter

The Colorado state quarter shows the Rocky Mountains. The quarter came out in 2006.

Glossary

dwellings (DWEL-ingz): Dwellings are places where people live. Cliff dwellings in Colorado were built into rock.

fossil (FOSS-ul): A fossil is the remains of an animal or plant that lived millions of years ago. Colorado's state fossil is the *Stegosaurus*.

manufacturing (man-yuh-FAK-chur-ing): Manufacturing is the task of making items with machines. Many people in Colorado work in manufacturing.

plains (PLAYNZ): Plains are areas of flat land that do not have many trees. Colorado has some plains.

plateaus (pla-TOHZ): Plateaus are flat areas on the tops of hills or mountains. Colorado has many plateaus.

popular (POP-yuh-lur): To be popular is to be enjoyed by many people. Skiing is a popular sport in Colorado.

resorts (rih-ZORTS): Resorts are places people go to relax and to do fun things. Colorado has many ski resorts.

seal (SEEL): A seal is a symbol a state uses for government business. Colorado's state seal has tools that stand for mining.

symbols (SIM-bulz): Symbols are pictures or things that stand for something else. The state seal and flag are Colorado's symbols.

tourism (TOOR-ih-zum): Tourism is visiting another place (such as a state or country) for fun or the jobs that help these visitors. Some people in Colorado work in tourism.

tribes (TRYBZ): Tribes are groups of people who share ancestors and customs. Native American tribes live in Colorado.

Further Information

Books

Miller, Amy. *Colorado*. New York: Children's Press, 2008.

Walker, Cynthia. *Colorado*. New York: Children's Press, 2004.

Whitney, Louise Doak. *C is for Centennial: A Colorado Alphabet*. Chelsea, MI: Sleeping Bear Press, 2002.

Web Sites

Visit our Web site for links about Colorado: *childsworld.com/links*

Note to Parents, Teachers, and Librarians: We routinely verify our Web links to make sure they are safe and active sites. So encourage your readers to check them out!

Index